CONTENTS

PART 01 IN THE BEGINNING

PART 02 THE INVISIBLE WORLD

PART 03 CREATING A CAPABLE CHARACTER

CONTENTS

PART 04 WHAT IF YOU COULD?

PART 05 WHAT ARE YOU WORTH?

No matter what your
dreams look like,
they are all the same,
a desire to return to

CHILD

Hey friend! I never wanted to sell or even write a book as much as I wanted to say something to the world. That something is kind of hard for me to explain directly, so I'm going to tell you a story that will help me illustrate it instead. That story is set in the 80s and 90s. It contains a little slice of life called my childhood. These childhood experiences form the backdrop I used to create the character known as Danny Valdes.

Then, I'm going to talk to you about a character that you may not even know you have created as well. It's the character that totally controls your life. This is a character that you designed and that you call "you." However, the "real" you is far more powerful than this character. The real you is waiting to be unleashed. I aim to do just that! We are going to do a deep dive into the question that will change everything.

So grab a mug of whatever it is you drink, get cozy, and let's head to Mexico!

01 IN THE BEGINNING

It was 1983 in Torreon Coahuila, Mexico. On the floor of his tiny, flat-roof house, a three-year-old boy was playing with his soccer ball. His mother, a beautiful, young, wild and pregnant American, was handwashing clothes and cranking them through the rollers of the wringer dryer. She hung them on the line in the hot Mexican sun. It's not that the sun was Mexican. It's that it presently was hanging over Mexico for the purposes of our story.

Now, this woman had been raised by a successful couple in a spacious, modern home in Youngstown, Ohio. She was far from home. The boy's father, a ravishing-looking Mexican, worked at a local market that his family owned. I guess it didn't work out down there in Aztec country, because the little family left Mexico for Memphis, TN. (Theme music stops.) I know, Memphis, right? No clue what brought that on. I will check with my mom on that and get back to you. (Theme music resumes.) So there we lived, in Memphis, in a tiny, tiny condo with—sorry, my mom just texted and said it wasn't Memphis but Pennsylvania, to live near her aforementioned successful parents and go to nursing school. That makes more sense now. My dad didn't go to Pennsylvania, though. He went to Memphis and worked as a plumber. He bought the tiny, tiny condo. After my brother was born and my mom finished nursing school, we moved to Memphis to be with my dad.

So Mom and Dad were back together, and we all lived in that condo on the East side, right across the street from East End Skating Center. Every Friday night, we would skate to Bryan Adams, Guns and Roses, and Salt-N-Pepa. Saturdays were kicked off with Lucky Charms, Voltron and Mario Brothers, which my grandma pronounced Mare-i-o Brothers.

It's weird—I remember a couple scenes from this time, but not a lot. I remember skating on Friday nights and running around the neighborhood in my underwear, perhaps a couple other crazy things, but not much. At some point during this time, my dad moved out but right into another condo in the same complex. We stayed with him on the weekends. We played Nintendo and ate Mexican food, and he had a roommate who punched a hole in the wall. I remember thinking, When I get stronger, I too want to punch a hole in a wall. Whenever we were playing video games and my dad lost, he would wail some sort of mysterious Spanish curses at the TV. My brother and I thought it was hilarious. We try and mimic it to this day, but it's really best coming from someone with the proper accent.

COMING UP

They say you're not fully a man until your daddy dies. My daddy died when I was eight. Well, not exactly. The idea of him died, I mean. He left. Vanished. I don't ever remember him driving away or anything. He just vanished one day when I wasn't there. Or maybe I was there. I could have been there but just not paying attention. I never paid attention. I had A. D. D.—Absent Dad Disorder. Either way, his vanishing was a non-event. He went back to Mexico, and I became an eight-year-old man.

A dad dying is better than a dad leaving. If your dad dies, your mom can tell you that "he loved you very much and he was a great man, and now it's your turn to carry the torch, etc." But a dad leaving, that's complicated. When a dad dies, a child is left with honor. When a dad leaves, a child is left with shame. When a dad leaves, he takes with him all he could have given. All the knowledge of manhood a boy will need at every stage in his life. I was an orphan child, not even knowing that I didn't know what I ought to know. As a young man without a father, you might passionately believe in foolishness, and who would correct you? You really aren't sure how to be. The world laughs at you. You are strange in the world, and you don't know why.

Every child raised by a single parent has to overcome their orphan ways and learn to navigate the world. Some never do. I remember being in shock the first time I had to open a bank account. I didn't know what any of it meant. Ledgers, deposit slips, and insufficient-fund fees. Lots and lots of insufficient-fund fees. I remember calling the bank in disbelief: "You guys have made an accounting error. It says I have no money in there and I should pay a fee!"

Pathetic.

Fatherless.

I felt no conscious pain growing up. I didn't know what I never knew. I never thought about it. However, I could not escape the years of setbacks and learning things the hard way. I don't think that's necessarily bad. I would have my life no other way. This is almost cliché to say, but every part of my life has formed the person I'm delighted with today. Memphis was where I really "grew up." Man, if you were from Memphis, you had to fight. I have been in so many

11

fights. If the lighting is just so, you can see my crooked nose to this day, broken from a fight in the ninth grade. You want to know what the fight was about? I beat a guy in badminton in gym class so we had to fight. Actually, it was probably my trash talking throughout the whole game that led to the fight. It was just a way of life in Memphis. I fought white people, black people, fat people, skinny people, groups of people, and a stepdad or two. We trained for it, too. Creatine supplements and protein drinks, push-ups and practice against friends. You just never knew when you were gonna have to fight when you were livin' in the M-Town!

WAR

Things began getting worse. Before moving from Memphis to Nashville (the exodus), I was selling weed and carrying a gun around. Just picture it. Shaved head, pocket full of weed, and a gun in my waistband. I didn't think it was crazy. Just like putting on my pants. I put my pants on, then my gun, then my shirt, and went about my day—what a waste.

I think one of the best things that happened to me was getting robbed. I didn't know it at the time, but I was actually set up to get robbed (or "jacked" as we called it) by my "friends." Yeah, I had known Dory and Coug for years. We hung out all the time, crazy right? Welcome to Memphis. At the time, they were literally the only "friends" I had. We were parked at a new construction site, on the weekend, when no one was working. It was deep behind my neighborhood in East Memphis, and no one was anywhere close. We were far enough away from other houses that a gunshot might sound like a firecracker. Dory was in the driver seat, and Coug was in the front passenger seat. Coug asked to see my gun, and I said, "Sure."

Twenty seconds later the door was yanked open, and they pulled Coug out and put a Glock 9 mm to my temple. You know a Glock when you see one. I knew I was dead. You know how people say that before you die your life flashes before your eyes? I saw it all. My mom, my brother, my room and video games; my favorite food: macaroni and cheese. I was saying goodbye to it all. I took the last couple seconds to grieve and wonder how I got here. All three of us were lying on our faces and emptying our pockets. The bad guy was wearing a hoodie and had a blue bandana over his nose and mouth.

Wait, I was selling drugs and carrying a gun around. Maybe I was a "bad guy." Anyway, I told the bad guy that I hadn't seen his face and that he could let us walk off into the woods and that he would never get caught. I told him he didn't have to shoot us. I remember visualizing what it might feel like to be shot. I wondered if he would shoot me in the back of the head, or several times in the back. Either way, I was trying to make peace with the fact that, hopefully, it would be quick. I was a fifteen-year-old soldier.

Pathetic.

Fatherless.

A car drove by. The bad guy hid behind our vehicle with the three of us on our faces. He told us that if we moved or said anything, we would be shot. I fooled myself with hope and thought, This car driving by surely must be my salvation! But it wasn't. They didn't seem to notice and kept driving. Bad guy took $600 from me, some weed, and my Sig Sauer .357 pistol. He jumped in Dory's car, drove down the street, and disappeared. We found Dory's car around the corner, and miraculously, none of his belongings were stolen. Just mine. I thought about that detail after the fact when relaying the story to another friend, who helped me confirm it was indeed a set-up.

I thought about retaliating. I thought more about how lucky I was to be alive. I mean, I wasn't shot. Here I am to write this story. I said it was one of the best things to ever happen, and in hindsight it was. It was a real wake-up call, and it kept me from going any deeper into the Memphis crime world where who knows what would have happened.

FLASHBACKS

I've lived a hundred lives. Up until recently, I had reoccurring dreams that someone was chasing me with a gun or that my life was in some other kind of grave danger. Maybe I've shaken them, but I don't know. I had PTSD for several years after I left that crazy Memphis scene. You ever heard of it? PTSD is a ferocious beast. God made me fight him. In the shower or when I was alone, I would picture events from my past. I would find myself right in the middle of the fight where my nose was broken. But this time, in my mind, I blocked the punch, spun around on the guy and— well, never mind.

Sometimes, when walking alone, I would stop suddenly in my tracks and, in my mind, be back in the gym locker room in a different fight. Well, if you can call that a fight. There I was, head in the floor urinal, getting kicked in the face and body by six guys. Back in real time, sweat would form on my forehead and clenched fists. This time, in my mind, I'm going to take them all on! If no one was around, I would swing at the air, attempting to fix the past, win the fight, and avoid being hurt. I was one of those crazy flashback guys! But I was friendly; the life of the party. I wasn't dangerous or anything. I just had emotional scarring that I dealt with anytime my mind was quiet.

Sometimes, when I was alone with my thoughts, I would flash to other painful memories. Like this one time I got beat down by one of my stepdads. I was a mouthy young man, and I must have said something to my stepfather to set him off. He punched me in the jaw, and I found myself on my back while he rained down fists. When I got up, I made my mind up that I had to kill him. It seemed like the logical thing to do. I MUST kill this man. He can't go on, and the universe is calling me to do it. Strangely, it wasn't an emotional decision. I didn't run wildly down the hall of our house looking for revenge. I calmly walked into my room, shut the door, reached under my mattress, and got my loaded gun. I turned around and headed toward my stepfather, ready to finally bring justice to the world.

As I reached for the handle of my bedroom door, something stopped me. In my mind, I pictured metal doors, steel bars, baloney sandwiches, and unsavory individuals with intense teeth. Prison life flashed before my eyes. If I do this then that will be where I will live...forever. I put my gun away. Nothing happened, and we never talked about it. Instead of firing my pain back at my stepfather, I absorbed it into my identity. My mind baked it into my self-worth. I saw myself as a worthless person who deserved beatdowns and abandonment. Life proved that to me over and over.

DANNY DIVES OUT WINDOWS

When I was fifteen, my mom and stepdad finally moved my brother and new sister and me out of wild Memphis and to sunny farming-town, Franklin, TN. "Aw, mom, there are cows everywhere! We're in hick town!" Thank God for hick town though. It was a much more peaceful place. Well, for most people. I, of course, managed to find the fringe. In no time, I was selling weed and running from party to party. At this point, school was irrelevant, and I only checked in there a couple times a year. I wanted to be drunk and high with friends at all times. If we weren't high, we were looking for weed.

As a "dealer" I kind of had a target on my back. All the poor and disillusioned people wanted what I had in my pockets: weed and money. I was at a party, and a couple of "friends" set me up again. I guess there are bad guys in middle Tennessee as well as in Memphis. I should have paid attention when they kept feeding me free liquor and things got blurrier and blurrier. Next thing I knew, I was in a bathroom with two huge guys (or was I a tiny guy?). They were brothers. Big, ugly brothers, just like in the movies.

One of them pinned my arms behind my back while the other went to work. The next scene I remember was waking up on the bathroom floor with empty pockets. I ran out of the house trying to find them, but they were gone, taking with them the last bit of trust I had in "friends." I found out later that they did that for payback from a previous event. Payback is what happens if you mess with someone who has friends in low places. So, do you want to hear about that previous event?

DANNY GETS RUN OVER

Like I said, we were always getting high or looking for weed. Two friends and I met a "cannabis salesman," as they are called today, and his driver at a market in Franklin. Back then, they were called "drug dealers." I got out with the money and got in the dealer's SUV for the exchange. Here was a fellow known for bad decisions and violence, like me. There I was getting into his vehicle. Two misdirected young men and their driver. The trio pulled out of the market and drove down the dark country road away from town. I was in the backseat with the dealer while my friends followed in the car behind. Dealer dude wanted the money first. I wanted the weed first. "How about the same time?" I suggested. He wasn't having it. Then he snapped—"Man, give me the money!"—and reached for my pocket.

Boy, we went at it! I'll save you the details, but he did not get the money. The driver pulled the SUV over but then tried to take off right as I was stepping out. The vehicle drove up the side of my leg, and the back wheel was a foot or two off the ground, resting on my knee. If the vehicle had kept going, it would have run me over completely, but strangely, it stopped. I simply stood up and it backed off my leg. It felt like one of those bizarre feats of unexplainable human strength. I can't explain how that happened. I'm not saying it was a miracle. Maybe the driver stopped and backed up. I really don't know, but why would one drug dealer show another that courtesy? I just calmly walked back to my friends' car. They had followed us during the whole event. My knee started to throb about ten minutes later, and by the time we were home, I couldn't put pressure on my foot to walk. An ER trip later and I was walking around with crutches and a leg brace, but even that didn't stop me from jumping out of windows to run from the police.

I was actually known for successfully evading arrest all the time. People would come up to me at parties or punk rock shows and say, "I heard everyone went to jail except you dove out the window." I would be like, "Yep."

I remember three parties in particular. At all three, literally everyone went to jail except me. I would wait until the police were inside and then hang-drop out of an upstairs window. Two of the times I did this, I hid in a nearby bush and watched just about everyone I knew getting loaded up into police cars. Each time I would precipitate from a party window, I would fervently pray, "God, if you get me out of this, I will never party again." Actually, come to think of it, I think my friend Dave (not his real name) jumped with me once. (Why is Dave always the "not his real name" name?) There we were, in the bush. I think I was schooling him in the art of not saying anything and holding still in a bush. Please do me a favor and picture two teens in 1990s suburbia, quaking in shrubbery and praying for deliverance. I'm laughing right now remembering all this. On and on I could go. Anyway, the big, ugly brothers from the bathroom incident were paying me back for my little backseat issue with their bud.

CREATING THE CHARACTER

There, now you have a snapshot of the backdrop. From this input, I created a street-smart character who was capable of surviving in harsh climates. That's just what I did until I discovered the truth. I only survived in a harsh environment. It was the climate I was used to. I grew up, took on a survivor persona, and created a life of struggle. I thought that life was hard, but really I was now subconsciously creating difficulty around me. This is hard to explain. As a child, struggle happened to me. Now, it was happening because of me.

MY DREAM GIRL

Now we must pause that story and interject with a love

tale as old as the foundations of the earth. I'm going to tell you how I found "the one," my soul mate. She was my star-crossed lover, set aside for me before time began—at least, that's how I see it. In spite of my character who struggled and made low-level, failing decisions, there was a shining light, a miracle that should not have happened, but did.

I was sitting downstairs at the entrance of a church I was attending at the time. Lots of people were walking in, and I, a friendly guy, said hello to most of them. So far, everything was normal. Then, everything was not normal. In walked a blonde girl. She was wearing a baggy shirt, dirty, grungy jeans with holes, and red skater shoes. She looked like a lost member of Nirvana. She seemed like a girl whom the world had pushed down and kicked a time or two.

I didn't have romantic feelings for her, but I did have a very strong, different kind of feeling. She felt like one of my kind. It was like she was my childhood best friend or my sister but we were separated long ago. I can't describe it, but she was so familiar. I went up to her immediately and introduced myself. She looked so cool. I wanted to be her friend instantly.

She started hanging around that church, and I saw her from time to time. I didn't feel for her, but I was glad she was there. I just always noticed her, but I never really talked to her. I noticed her spirit, I mean. It's like I loved her but didn't know it. She wasn't just a pretty girl. She was a special being. Ah, this is so hard to describe. Have you ever been out of the country to a place that doesn't speak your language? You feel so out of place until you hear someone speaking English. You run up to them and have an immediate bond because they are from where you are from. It was like that. I was an alien, and this girl was from my planet. Her name was Lisa.

I always thought, Man, some lucky guy is gonna get the greatest girl ever made. It will probably be some deep, guitar-playing hippy who knows how to make a girl dream. I knew she was way above my level, and I was at a place where I was not interested in dating anyone. Everyone around me was dating and breaking up and it all looked so dramatic. I had made a pact with God. I told him that an angel would have to come to me in the night and with flaming sword reveal to me the woman I should marry, or something just as clear. The decision of who to marry was too big, and I was too afraid to just make that call. I told God that it would have to be a divine revelation or I would assume I would be single the rest of my life because I was not looking anymore.

Lisa and I had known each other about a year when one day, she was just standing there talking, and something epic happened. A strange knowing blasted me in the face. Everything made sense all at once. Every time I had ever seen her, everything I had ever felt, everything she had ever said, it was all in front of my mind at once. An angel didn't come in the night, but something did come just as clear. It was as if the heavens had opened and a clear knowledge that this was my wife was pounded into my understanding. It all made sense—she was indeed my soul sister! Now remember, we had only really had a few short conversations here and there. I had not had a chance to get to know this girl. All I had was my crazy idea that I might be the lucky hippie guy.

Although the heavens opened, I kept my secret to myself. After all, I can't just go up to a girl and say, It has been divinely revealed to me that thou shalt be my wife! At this point, this was merely a girl I saw at church once a week. Week after week I would see her, and I would be dying inside. I felt so strongly about her but I couldn't utter a word. I feared I would scare her away with such nonsense. So I did the charming thing. I awkwardly stared at her every week, searching for some clue from her that I was on the right track. Maybe she had a revelation too? Nothing. She just looked back at me like, What's this guy staring at? Then I would look away and go home. Gah, what a dork.

One night, everyone was leaving the church and I was giving her my usual charming, stalker gaze. She broke the silence. "Do we need to talk?"

My heart fell into my stomach! "I think so?" I mumbled. As the crowd dwindled, we paired off in the parking lot while her roommate waited in the car. It was already late. I went first. Now, what I am about to tell you took exactly one hour for me to say. I kept repeating myself and rephrasing, trying desperately to make her interrupt me and say it first. I was just stalling, waiting for some clue that I was on the right track. Nothing. I knew for sure that I was about to ruin everything but I had to do this. I said, "Look, if I'm wrong here, can we please just move on and pretend I said nothing? I mean, I just want to be friends forever and if me saying this ruins that then please don't go away. Please don't be awkward, because I'll be totally cool, I promise."

I would not have been totally cool. I would have been single the rest of my life. This was perfection, a dream come true, and if it wasn't real, then nothing would be. Everyone else seemed second-best compared to Lisa. On that night, I would rather have had Lisa in my life and her marry the other luckiest guy in the world than to lose her completely. I would have her even as a friend, if it meant not losing her.

I wanted to give her everything. I truly wanted nothing in return. If we could just sail away and be best friends and go on adventures forever, that would be enough. I was drawn to her, it seemed, without reason.

I continued, "I feel like everyone on Earth is on a two-person boat. Each of these boats are going out in a separate direction. They are all going to something unique and specific, and there is only room for two. Now, I don't know how to explain this, but everything in me wants to say—I feel like you're on my boat." I stopped talking ,and with bulging, wide eyes, stared back at her for what seemed like ninety-eight hours exactly.

She broke the silence. "I ... feel ... the same way." It was not a dream! I was the lucky hippy! She told me that she had loved me since the day I said hello to her at the church entrance. She thought that she was crazy and that I would marry some lucky, preppy, cheerleader type. Can we just have a big LOL right now?

What if you could lay out an impossible standard to the heavens? What if you could say, "May I know clearly what action I should take." What if you could risk it all and say what you need to say? For all you know, the endless sky of potential will open up and you will get what you ask!

Lisa and I both come from generations of brokenness, pain, abuse and divorce and yet... the cycle has been broken! How and why do we get to be stowaways on the ship of life? Why have we created four souls on this planet together? Why do I get to be a father who pours love on his children, and they pour their love on me, day in and day out? No alcoholism, no abuse, and no divorce. The cycle had been broken, and the tree of life was bearing fruit. Why was I in the middle of this dream? Everything else in my life was failing, but this was miraculously succeeding. God help me, I'm weeping.

I left off saying that struggle was happening because of me. I was married to the girl of my dreams, living with the children of my dreams, but going from one garbage job to the next. It wasn't until my "I'll do it" moment that I broke out of the subconscious failure system that I created—but I'll tell you about that in a bit.

sub·con·scious
/səbkänSHəs/

adjective

"of or concerning the part of the mind of which one is not fully aware but which influences one's actions and feelings."

Out of this world, these formative years, I fashioned a character I believed to be me. I became a survivor without direction. Sounds like the title of a romance novel. It was the title of mine, minus the romance.

I remember the day I became an adult. It was when I had to pay my own bills. Fear of surviving in America made me a much more sensible and responsible creature. I put aside my childish light and took on the intensity of a man. A man trying to survive in America. No big deal to most, but to the pathetic and fatherless, overwhelming.

I wandered aimlessly through life, taking whatever the wind blew my way. I was not the designer of my life but merely an opportunist. If something good came my way, I would jump on it. I left everything up to chance or "God." I designed nothing, because I didn't believe I had that power.

Everything just blew into my view, and I either accepted or rejected it. Some years things were going great, and other years we were struggling. I was always doing my best, always praying, always trying to interpret the struggles of life.

There was a force in my life, kind of like gravity, always present and pulling me down. I had control of nothing. Outside forces blew me about. I was a ship with no rudder. This was my character's destiny. This was the character controlling my adulthood. Did I say outside forces? See, I'm still working on the habit of ownership. I meant inside forces. I was the force. I created the wind and shivered when it blew.

The subconscious, self-limiting work I built into myself happened without effort or even knowledge on my part. It was the inevitable effect, the atrophy of a survivor. The day I moved out of my mom's house and had to provide for myself (my first day of adulthood), I exchanged my imagination for responsibility. I entered the "real world" of safe decision-making. I made low-risk choices for the sake of security. Those low-risk choices were made from an unwritten yet very real handbook in my mind of how to do life. That handbook was written as I watched events unfold around me.

GARBAGE DAN

So, I was tired and unhealthy, working mediocre jobs for pitiful wages, never believing I had permission to do my thing—the thing I would do if I knew that no matter what I would succeed. The thing I did as a child. The thing I would do even if I knew it would fail. The thing I would do for its own sake, because it must be done.

So, I went from one low-level, garbage job to the next. I was never satisfied with my work, the thing for which I traded eight to fifteen hours a day! I didn't love my work, and so I didn't love my life. Every day, I hated most of the hours in the day, and I loved maybe four hours in the evening. My only consolation was the amazing family I had waiting for me at home. As the years went by, my frustration grew more and more, and I knew I was starting to bring that frustration home with me. Before I got out of my truck at the end of the workday, I would pray, "Help me leave this stress at work and come home with a good attitude." It wasn't enough. I couldn't focus at home when I was so miserable at work. I was at my house with my family but not present. I would look through my children rather than at them, and they would have to repeat themselves many times to get my attention. My mind was elsewhere, on a hamster wheel of thought, trying to figure out what my purpose was, what sort of work I should be doing, and how I was going to pay these bills. I was a self-employed carpenter, which at one point was my goal. I loved the independence, but the business itself was just a ball of headaches.

Work was getting low. Wait, was work getting low, or was I subconsciously not doing the things that would bring about work? Yes, that's it. I wanted out. So a certain Monday came, and I found myself without work that week. I sent emails, posted ads on Facebook and called contractors—nothing. Friday came, and I was done. Ever felt done? I felt terrible, because I loved my family more than anything in the world, but I was so—I don't know, without direction. I was ready to sell my house and live in a tent for the rest of my life. Perhaps then I could escape the stress of garbage jobs and garbage pay. There I was, in my woodworking shop on a Friday. No work and no hope. Pacing in circles and thinking about what a monument of unfulfilled potential I was. A failure with nothing to offer the world and no example to set for my children. My external condition was garbage. I didn't know it then, but I was soon to learn that my external state was simply mirroring my internal state. My identity: trash. An object to be used and thrown away. The face that life punches.

I was a self-employed, out-of-work carpenter. I was married with four kids and out of money. Angry and out of ideas, I paced circles in my woodworking shop. The thing I wanted most was hopelessly out of reach. I had proven it was impossible. For a while, I wondered when it was going to happen or if it was going to happen at all. Perhaps destiny will come. I felt trapped, trapped in my body and circumstances. *Maybe God's not real. Maybe I'm in the matrix.*

HOW TO SABATOGE

Then I met Brett. It was in a barn at a music festival at my friend's house in Tennessee. I was playing drums at this event, and Brett was managing a band called The Redhead Express. They needed a drummer, and he asked if I would go on their fall tour with them. I was out of work, so I said yes. Brett and I became great friends. We would often stay up till 4 a.m. talking about life, space, God, and whatever. On that tour, I was reminded of how much I loved the entertainment industry. My entire childhood was spent getting in the center of rooms and making people laugh.

In high school, the only class besides science I loved was theatre arts. Somewhere along the way, sometime around the misdirected party years, that love was lost. After the tour, I decided that I wanted to pursue the Nashville music industry. Through too many miracles to tell you about, I received an invite to meet with the head of the record label

Big Loud Records to talk about a tour manager position. What!? Here was my break. So there I was in downtown Nashville, in the waiting room of a big, fancy office building with gold records all over the walls. I was called in, and thus my meeting with one of the lords of the music industry commenced. He offered me five times my income and asked, "Will that work for you?"

I responded without gulping, "Yeah I think so," trying my best to look like a guy who gets offers like this all the time. "...but the time commitment away from my family feels a little much," I added. I told him I would get back with him after I gave it some thought.

That afternoon, I called Brett to tell him how the meeting went. I told him my comment about the time commitment away from family. He screamed. "What! But you might have to sell your house! You are miserable with work and wanting change. You made it to the inner circle of the music industry, and you blew it! If you hate it, you can quit in six months or level up to a more balanced position. You, Danny, are a professional at self-sabotage!" At the time, I had never heard the expression. He continued, "You claim you want success in your life, but deep down in your identity, you think you are garbage."

I responded, "Am I not protecting my family?"
Brett howled, "No! You are protecting your own low self-worth. In your mind, you're not worth a job you love. You're not worth a life where you don't have to struggle, fight and suffer. You want to confirm that you are worthless. You are your own self-fulfilling prophecy."

Was he right? Should I listen to another man tell me how to provide for my family? "What if you're wrong and this is going to ruin my life?" I asked. I was panicking.

"Danny, this is a big blind spot for you. I can see this so clearly. I've been right where you are. I want you to do something probably for the first time in your life. I want you to trust someone else. I want you to trust me. You need to go back there right now and tell him you'll take the job. You need to take care of your family, Danny."

I'LL DO IT

Silence.
Brett pushed forward, "Hello?"
I responded, "I'm here."
"Well?" he said.

Silence.

I was pacing and sweating. Terrified of what might happen. Terrified that I would abandon my family for the pursuit of money. This is what I feared. That my children would grow up without a father. Brett wouldn't let up. "Commit right now. Tell me you'll do it." I don't remember how long I just sat there in silence, choking fear coiling around my throat, a fist squeezing my heart. The feeling of losing my grip on a thousand-foot ledge—stabbing, relentless fear.

Out it came, nonetheless, "I'll do it."

The label was already closed for the day, so after a sleepless night, I drove back up to the hall of golden records. The lord of country music was surprised to see me. I told him the commitment would not be a problem and that I would like to accept the job. But he had already made up his mind to give it to another person. He said I wasn't the right fit. He made his mind up the second I showed reservation in the interview. You should know I have zero regrets. The second-most-significant breakthrough of my life happened when I told Brett, "I'll do it." Brett didn't care that I didn't get the job either. He celebrated the breakthrough with me. That was the point. I stopped pursuing the practical, low-risk work that would guarantee income but also unfulfillment, and started pursuing the dangerous work I was passionate about and secretly wished I could do!

I was riding on a new high in my life. I wasn't scared anymore. I wasn't afraid of losing my family or my house. I let go of the fear that I thought was protecting my family and me. I finally put bold action behind my purported desires. I learned what it looked like to see opportunity and act decisively. I stopped projecting my abandonment onto my family. They are never going to lose their daddy!

I wasn't afraid of being rejected or not good enough and, interestingly, I no longer needed other people to fulfill me or help me in any way. I wasn't waiting on fortune's favor, or a surprise check in the mail to save me anymore. In one breakthrough moment, I was in control. I finally took ownership over my life and what I had built and accepted the truth that I can accomplish anything I want. I can go after things or I can not. If I'm half-hearted, the world will sense it and, for reasons unknown to them, not want to work with me. Hire someone else. They'll say, "It wasn't the right fit." I took ownership. I was the writer of my story now.

THAT REALLY DEEP DOWN FEELING

A survivor's mentality (paying bills, getting by, putting food on the table) did not serve me. "Survival" provided false comfort. "Pet me and live," is the claim. I mean, the survival instinct is brilliant. It keeps us from falling off cliffs or driving too fast. However, survival can be a big source of frustration. You know, walking the prudent, responsible, safe path leaves no room for the imagination and no room for life. But I was on a new path now. I had to re-awaken the ability to imagine and pursue what felt like absurdities. I asked, "What do I deep down really want even if it feels silly saying it?"

I remember kids in school talking about wanting to be a fireman or a mom or a nurse. When it was my turn to answer the question about what I wanted to be when I grew up, I always said, "astronaut." I didn't mean that I wanted to actually do the work to become an astronaut (ugh ... to think of the math alone), I just wanted to identify as an astronaut, zooming around the galaxy and floating in space. Looking back, I probably wanted to just leave my world. The message I learned about adulthood was scary. "Pretty soon all the fun and games are going to be over, and it will be time to be serious. You will need to decide what you want to be when you grow up. On career day, you will take a look at the professions you see around you and pick one."

There was a problem with that. I didn't want to be any of those things I saw on career day. Think about the mind freak we set up. "Pretty soon you'll have to survive. Here are some ways to do that. Choose wisely!" Why do I have to be something else if I want to survive in the real world? But there was the problem of money. So I started doing things I could do to make money, i.e. carpentry and stuff that didn't require school, things I could learn on my own. (Did I mention I left school in the 10th grade?)

Again, I had to face deep fear and get real. What did I deep down want to do with my life, no matter how silly it sounded? What if I really could be anything I wanted to be? Isn't that what the grown-ups promised us as kids? Since I was a child, I was always in the middle of a room, making the group laugh or getting into trouble. Before I had to survive, I was one way, and now I was another. Survival was blocking me from seeing what was in my heart. What did I really, really want in my life? I couldn't put my finger on it. Whenever I came close to what I really, really wanted, a voice in my head would scream ridicule.

The voice was right: it was absurd. You know those people who really can't sing, but they go on American Idol and embarrass themselves? It's clear to everyone watching that they suck at singing, but they have such hope in their eyes. Then the judges tell them, "Sorry Candice the dancing comedian, but you suck," and they go back to their real life. I was horrified that I was going to be one of those people, that I would one day have to go back to my real life. It would be too much to bear that the fantasy would be over and destiny would prove that hc could not be beaten ... but I kept moving forward. I had to find out. I didn't know exactly what I was getting into, but I knew I loved people, I loved stories, and I loved to make people laugh with stories.

My headspace was so different now. I was actually going for what I wanted, and for the first time it seemed the world wanted what I wanted. I wasn't begging and bidding for work anymore—people were reaching out to me. What sort of magic was this? Around this time is where Trim Healthy Mama enters the picture. My good friends wrote a book that changed the way people approach dieting and health. It became a bestseller, and they built a product company around their message. One of the author's husbands (Sam) called me and invited me for coffee. See, I had worked with Sam in the past. We were both in the trade industry, him as a painter and me as a carpenter. We were great friends and always got along famously. Sam somehow found out about my entertainment pursuits and said they had some media projects coming in the future. He wondered if I would be interested in being a part of their new company. About a year later, the Trim Healthy Mama authors, Serene and Pearl, started a podcast and invited me to be a host on the show, "The Trim Healthy Podcast." I accepted. It was right in line with the exciting new direction of my life.

That same year, I contacted an actors agency in town, and they wanted me to send in an audition tape. They wanted three monologues. I looked up some of my favorite actors on YouTube and made an iPhone video of me acting out their scenes. It felt so silly. Who am I to think I have what it takes to be an actor? But I've been an actor my whole life. Armed with a tenth-grade degree, I faked my way into over twenty jobs. Also, I realized that everyone is an actor anyway. In the drama that is life, I was playing the character that begged and didn't succeed. My character type was not written to break through and do incredible things on his own. He was not the "leading man," as the film industry calls it.

So, absurdly, I began acting. My over-the-top personality found a resting place in front of the camera. Acting is one of the hardest things I have ever done, yet somehow it's quite natural as well. I mean, it's a perfect fit, but it demands all of me. Time flies when I'm on set, and I'm never more alive. When I'm acting, I lose track of everything else. I don't care about social media or what other people are doing with their lives. I'm fully present and in that moment. It's as if I were made for it, this shapeshifting into other characters. Acting was the secret thing I wanted and also the thing I was most terrified to pursue. Yet I was armed with my question, "What if I could?" and so I did. I began auditioning and landing commercial and film roles. My little magical question was changing everything, and absurdities were coming true.

Where exactly is the line between absurd and practical? I have found that the things I called absurd last year are now this year's normal. I just needed to stretch. My will to survive really got in the way. I allowed it to go past usefulness in establishing basic needs. It dominated my goals and dreams. It was time to use a different part of my brain, the imagination. When I moved out of my mom's house, I asked, "How will I pay my bills, where will I live, and how will I eat?" When we think about what we want to accomplish in our lives, our careers or our health goals, we have to ask different questions. Especially if what we want is impossible. New, high-risk questions must be asked. Questions like, "What do I want more than anything?" and "Who will I choose to be in this world?" These questions help us get to the root of our goals in life.

Let me ask you an old question. If you could snap your fingers and make literally anything at all happen for you in an instant, what would you wish? What if you could create a healed relationship, a new body, or a fantastic career doing your favorite thing? Write it down. Anything? I learned that there was a way to make these impossible things happen. My bigger obstacle, however, was not knowing if I should make them happen. I remember when I was afraid that I would step out of line or something if I went for what I was passionate about. I had to stay "humble" and "wait on God's timing." I had a golden wheelchair that kept me from walking. If anything was going to happen in my life, it had to come as a surprise miracle. In my mind, it was either destined to happen or it shouldn't. I was not the kind of man who just made things happen. Well, my character wasn't that kind of man. But what if I could be that kind of man?

I began to ask myself, aren't other people living this very thing that I deem impossible? Did they have more resources than me when they started out? Most did not. In fact, the opposite is more often true. Many of the most outrageously remarkable successes in this world have been wrought by people who had the most disadvantages by far. People who were so poor and at such a deficit that all they had was their imagination, belief and willpower. No money, no contacts, bad metabolism, abusive parents, no arms, no legs, etc. Literally, the only asset they had was their brain. Well, don't I have a brain? It was time to put it to work.

I had to make a hard choice to believe without sight. My new approach to life didn't feel right at first. It went against my programming. I had to get used to my powerful, future-creating self and avoid sabotaging. Good mentors come in handy on this point. I learned to surround myself with people already succeeding at doing what I wanted, even if I had to pay them for their coaching or time. They held me accountable and encouraged my new ability to see and create what I wanted in my life. They also challenged me when I reverted back to my garbage-creating mentality.

Beneath your conscious mind, deep within the infamous subconscious, lies a network of thoughts and beliefs, built one upon another, taking all of your life to knit into what you now call "you." You so deeply identify with this character. You can't imagine not being this character. You rejoice when this character succeeds and grieve when this character fails. You genuinely feel for this character. This character is good at some things and bad at others, in your mind, according to the rules you made, according to the script you wrote.

A voice is calling out to you, a voice from the future, your future. Your future does exist. It's almost here, and how it will look is up to you. There is a powerful voice calling Imagine yourself, in the future, experiencing the success

34

of the work you put in today. Imagine future you looking back at you in the now. What would future you tell you right now? I'm saying "future" but I don't mean it like you think.

02 THE INVISIBLE WORLD

Destiny is what happens no matter what, right? The concept of destiny is that no matter what sort of action you take, what is meant to happen will happen. It's out of your hands and can't be controlled. If you were meant to be a farmer, then you will, for sure, be a farmer. You don't need to take ownership or take any action. What's going to happen is going to happen no matter what you do.
I had to get real. That is not the sort of universe in which we live. Destiny and fate were hiding places for my fear. My butler's name was destiny. He helped me prop up my feet and relax. He placed a remote in one hand and bag of chips in the other. I thought he was such a great servant and friend, but he is no friend. He waits for you to do nothing and die so he can eat you in the end.

THE INVISIBLE FORMS THE VISIBLE

And now we must tune our attention to matters of space, science and the great beyond, the future which is happening now. In reality, the future doesn't exist, only the un-created. When are you ever in the future? Never. You are always in the present. And presently, you are merely taking actions which will lead to outcomes which will create more actions by you which will create more outcomes. The future isn't coming. You are designing it. In fact, you are currently living in a "future" that you designed years ago. Whether accidental or on purpose, you designed it. Welcome to the eternal realm of limitlessness!

Check this word out, entelechy. Aristotle made up this word. It speaks of the realization or actualization of potential. We talk of potential as something possible but that does not yet exist. But what if this potential is actually a thing? What if, undetected by our senses, this potential is buzzing about, unseen to the naked eye, waiting to "assemble," so to speak? The things we can see don't come from non-existent things. Before a rock formed, the particles that made up that rock could have taken many other forms. Perhaps these protons, neutrons and electrons could have smashed themselves into aluminum atoms or maybe formed into the hydrogen that would help make a raindrop. The particles had potential to be many things, but circumstances and forces (entelechy) pressed them into an actual rock. They moved from the realm of the possible to the realm of the actual. The sub-atomic world of the tiny takes shape and becomes a detectable reality to observe and hold. But wait, the particles are actually things themselves. So potential is not a theory, it's just a description of a smaller, yet very real world. A particle is a particle, no matter how small.

The way our universe works is fascinating. Especially the quantum universe. The quantum universe is the space in which matter and energy exist in the form of atoms and even smaller particles. The word "quantum," by definition, is a "discreet quantity of energy." The energy is discreet but not lacking in power. Remember, the biggest bombs known to man are built with this discreet energy. These tiny things are the building blocks of all that we can observe. From starlight to babies, it's all made of quantum energy! In the quantum or "tiny" world, mind-blowing energy is stored in tiny bits of matter or particles. They combine to form planets, solar systems, and humans! They fashion your very thoughts and ideas. Even physics experts don't understand all the implications that the quantum world has on the world we can see. What if you could go quantum?

LET'S GET WEIRD

At the most fundamental or quantum levels of reality, anything is possible. Here we find teleportation, entangled particles, time travel, and unlimited creation. The potential is endless. I began to wonder if the basic stuff that makes up everything we know has this freedom and power, and if our reality is framed on these building blocks, might that be an indicator of what is possible for human reality as well? Aren't our minds and bodies made of these tiny, limitless things? True, with current technology we cannot teleport (as far as I know), but we should not say teleportation is impossible. We simply can't do it as of this writing. Currently, we have the electron microscope and the atom bomb, to name two examples of harnessing the quantum world. Remember, the light bulb was invented not too long ago. As we advance in science, we will be more and more able to harness these "invisible" powers. But that's not my point.

My point is that if that is the type of universe we live in, why would that limitlessness cease to matter when it comes to our reality? From particles to planets, this invisible world, according to science, profoundly matters. Why not the space between? Why not us? Scientifically speaking, everything connects to everything. The hidden world has everything to do with the world we can detect. If we zoom into our brains, we find electrons, protons, leptons, quarks, and all of them in a flurry of limitless movement and action! These quantum building blocks are the stuff that knit us together. Limitlessness itself floats about our brain and makes us who we are. What would your life look like if you believed that you were limitless? What would your life look like if you not only believed that nothing was impossible, but you took action on those beliefs?

TRAINING FOR LIMITLESSNESS

"Quarks" are said to be one of the fundamental building blocks of all there is. When they combine, they make bigger particles that eventually make, for example, the neurons whereby your thoughts travel about your brain. Even as you read this, quarks are flying around your mind, responding to this information. Scientists say that their behavior is much like human thought. They don't act like the kind of matter which obeys the rules of classical physics. Instead, they behave like thoughts, seemingly undecided and flexible. They take some path to their end, then cycle back to try another route. Sometimes they combine to form particles. Other times they resist smashing together and just soar around the quantum world, waiting to become something new. It's like they exist everywhere. They seem to be potential itself, waiting to come into the actual! But they are the actual as well. They are an invisible power, and things begin to exist when they interact.

There are other particles called neutrinos. They are so small that they can pass through your body without so much as touching another atom. It's as easy for them to do this as it would be for you to walk through a mile-wide door. If we could strap a tiny camera on these particles and watch as they passed through your body, we would not be able to see blood vessels, platelets or even cells. We would be too small. Perhaps in the foggy distance, we would see an iron atom floating about. I don't know. How could I know? I'm not that tiny.

Remember when I told Brett, "I'll do it?" Something happened that was more than just changing my mind. At that moment. a shockwave went through my brain. Physical things actually happened. A plow fell into the hard, dry ground. New seeds were buried and watered. Possibility quarks were combining into thoughts. Those thoughts were firing down neuron pathways and locking in "states of mind." My quantum brain took part in the symphony where billions upon billions of tiny particles began to play together, expand my beliefs, and crescendo in my life. Our brains, along with the entire universe, are framed upon potential and held together with what physicists call "The Force."

USE THE FORCE

You will believe something about yourself, and you will subconsciously take action. You already have. As you were growing up, endless potential was swirling around you at all times. There were so many things you could have been and so many paths you could have taken. The open sky of potential was before you. At some point, from the realm of all possibility, this potential turned into an "actual," and you began building the very life you experience today. Look around you. What have you made? You have taken some paths, and you have not taken others, just like a thought in a neuron, just like a quark. Your brain paths turned into life paths. As you were growing up, you were deciding who you were going to be based on the things you came to value. It's just science.

For teenagers, this process can be stressful. At some point, we set our minds to believe an idea about what we are. And whatever we believe is what we will bring into our life or reality. Our identity will feel genuine and authentic, but it's just acting. Some will say, "That's just the way things turned out in my life." But they could have easily chosen another identity, another way of life, so long as their values and conclusions were as fixed and determined. "Things" don't just "turn out" in our life. For the most part, they are created by us.

"I am" ... a doctor.
"I am" ... a homeschool mom. "I am" ...

Some people will believe what they think they are, deep in their heart, their core. They will own it and be unable to see its construct. And so they commit to an identity about themselves and build a life based on the abilities of the character whom they call "me." Identity is a powerful force. From it, you built everything you see around you. So "Who am I?" is the wrong question. It suggests that destiny has fixed our position. The reality is, you are who you choose to be.

You are where you are today because of your potential, your beliefs, and the actions you took. You see, you can do anything. At some point in your past, you wanted what you have today. Remember that? Remember wanting what you have today? You may not be happy with what you have, but believe this, you created it. I'm not talking about material possessions. You can create anything, and you've already proven that. It may be hard, but try and trace back your steps and remember the actions you took to build what you currently have. See, it wasn't magic. It was art, and you created it. When we aren't happy with our art, it's usually because it was made without us knowing that we were making it. In other words, we made it unconsciously and not as part of a purposeful plan. We thought we were just "living life." Not so, little artist. Your whole life is one art piece created by you. It's just like oil on canvas. What if you could open your eyes when you paint? You may have done your creation unconsciously up until now, but merely responding and reacting to what may come is the quickest path to being disappointed. It's just surviving. I used to be a responder, never knowing that I was allowed to be a creator. In my mind, such talk was akin to usurping the throne of God.

Sometimes the things we want most, we can't seem to reach. One reason for this is that we aren't sure it wants us, metaphorically speaking. And so because we are afraid we won't get it, we either don't try, or faux try in a way that sabotages it from really happening. In other words, we don't believe. In this state, there is no way in the known universe that you can achieve what you are after. However, trapped inside is another person who can do this impossibility. Not only that, you should do it! All of humanity is waiting for the unique expression that is you. If you don't do it, the puzzle won't be complete. We need you.

TIME TRAVEL

Future you is calling. Future you lives in the realm of all possible outcomes based on actions you take, which flow out of who you are being today. I know, that last sentence was a mouthful. But it is my daily meditation. A person with powerful beliefs who is taking action will see impossibilities yield to their will. I've read too many books only to be inspired but not see any change or breakthroughs in my life. They were inspirational but not transformational. Transformation is a slower, more deliberate process. That process is empowered by the beliefs you choose to have and the actions you take. Belief is a choice. You can choose to believe anything you want. And when you couple that belief with action, mountains will move for you. Don't just believe, take relentless action, and make things happen. Belief without action is dead.

Whenever we first set out to create new realities, we will often have thoughts about our capabilities. "Who am I kidding? I'm such a faker." The reason for this is a bad habit that we must all overcome. It's the bad habit of looking in the wrong places to find answers to these questions. There are two places, by default, where we most often look: the past and the present. Makes sense, right? I mean, we can't see the future, can we?

Yes, we can. We are time travelers! Let us go forward in time into the future realm of all possible outcomes. Then we can come home to the present, take action, and bring about the future we saw.

So, when we ask the question, "What is possible?" we often look to the past to find out what others have done before. Then we look around us in the present. We wonder what others are currently doing in an attempt to find the system or template that we can apply to our lives. We want to copy them. If we see another person with two arms and two legs doing something, we assume we must be able to as well. But what if you could look into the future? I can tell you exactly how to see the future. You, little time traveler, will decide what it will be. Think about your future. What do you see? There. That's it! You just saw the future! You will (subconsciously) create what you just saw. Did you like what you saw? If not, create a new mental picture, and make sure it's epic!

CHANGING THE MENTAL PICTURE

At first, it felt like faking, but I had to change and become a different person somehow. My past had to mean something different, and I needed to be different to move forward. I'm not talking about the real me, by the way. I'm talking about the "identity" me. Character work is hard. It's hard to change who you think you are. Sometimes, a simple action can get our brains shifting in the right direction. Little exercises can address who you are being, not simply what you are doing. People want to know what they need to do differently. To go to new places, we have to be different; then, the doing will happen subconsciously, effortlessly, without our trying. You'll always do the right thing when you become the right person for this job. We did this naturally as children, then adulthood happened.

If you have achievable goals, then all you need to do is work hard. You probably don't need to read through the rest of this book. Just go get it, tiger. This book will be an adventure into the deeper work required to do impossibilities. It's for people who need massive change. I lived with a frustrated destiny until I learned to unseat the identity responsible for me not being where I wanted to be.

Similarly, if the thing you are trying to do is impossible, then that means that you cannot do it. So you cannot continue as you are, nor can you work harder. You must change who you are. Then you will inevitably take the right kind of action. That is what unlocks impossibilities. We're talking about being vs. doing. Continuing down this path will, at times, feel like one fight after another. That's part of why I wrote this book. I don't want that to be a surprise for you, and more importantly, I don't want you to give up under any circumstances. I want the phrase "What if you could?" to be burned into your being. Every time you begin to doubt yourself or make excuses, the question should rise, "But what if I could?"

FUTURE YOU

"Future me lives in the future realm of all possible outcomes based on actions I take which flow out of who I am being today."

Break it down into segments and think about each one.

Future Me
The realm of all possible outcomes
Actions I take
Who I am being today

You and I have a piece of God to give the world. A message or idea is in you, needing to be set free. May you be a unique expression of what's possible, releasing your full potential on the earth.

PART 03 CREATING A CAPABLE CHARACTER

Scene 1 - Take 1 - ACTION!

FADE IN:
INT. BATHROOM - MORNING
Background sound FX: Kids playing in the background.
Water running.

Scene opens. The character "Danny" is standing in front
of the mirror, straightening his tie and lamenting the
new hair growing between his eyebrows. He practices his
handshake to himself in the mirror.

Danny

Hello. (Extends hand for a handshake. Smiles confidently).
I'm Danny Valdes. Nice to meetcha! No no, too intense for
a first meeting. Try again. Hello, I'm Danny Valdes, and
you are?"

THE REAL YOU

I always practiced my lines. This was my habit before
going to a party or a dinner. I would rehearse the inevitable

moment of meeting someone for the first time. In front of the mirror, I would shake hands with an invisible someone and introduce myself. Sometimes I would rehearse saying "goodbye" in a memorable way—such a big act. I would look in the mirror, at my body and face, but through an applied overlay of beliefs about myself. My eyeballs were seeing a body, but my mind and body were re-affirming an idea. This idea wasn't something I could describe on paper but rather more of a feeling. Sometimes it felt confident, occasionally ashamed. Sometimes I would feel like a powerful businessman, other times a failure. Sometimes I would mildly squint at myself and say in my mind, "There goes a dapper individual," and other times, "Who do you think you're kidding?" I entered each day playing out the role I wrote for myself. This role, this identity, was not created quickly. I meticulously and subconsciously designed this role throughout my life. So subtle and detailed, in fact, that I called the current me my authentic self. "Me." The mirror is just for maintenance. It's like oiling the identity machine.

By about our mid-to-late twenties, we lock this character in place. The hard-working farmer with principles, or perhaps the bubbly, talkative and creative mom? I was the no-nonsense, tough carpenter. But why are our existing habits and ways (personality) so authentic? What is it that makes you ... you? Is it because you've been practicing your ways for so long that you call it "the way you are?" How many years do you have to be a certain way for it to qualify as authentic? How long until you can claim, "this is the real me?" I'm asking you, "Who is the real you?" Aren't they just the person you've created?

So why can't you come up with a person, a persona, who can do the impossible thing you want to accomplish? This person would be a specialist in this area, someone capable of pulling it off.

YOUR FORMATIVE YEARS

Oh, the teen years! Did anyone else have multiple horrifyingly awkward years of self-introspection? Were you embarrassed or did you have butterflies around members of the opposite sex? Do you remember feeling like a wimp while everyone around you was strong? Do you remember having an ugly face while everyone else's face was beautiful? Were any of those things true, though? I don't think that they were true or false, but merely our interpretation of reality based on our beliefs about ourselves.

Some teens will misinterpret their social anxiety. Some will believe, for example, that they don't do well in large crowds. But others will believe that when they enter a room, their job is to be in the center of that room, perhaps make that whole room laugh. Oh, how I remember how horrible my teen years sometimes were, just a constant feeling of inadequacy. I was always comparing myself to others. If I saw a character trait in someone that I liked, I would mimic them and behave like them. Do your children do this? When they return from playing with kids who are buck-wild, have they picked up some habits?

That's one of the moments I'm talking about right there, the moment that a child directs their brain to be something new. To take on a new persona. Persona is a word with Latin origins. It means to be a character in a play. To put on a mask. It's where we get the word person. All children do this subconsciously. They are quite willing to make alterations to their self in order to fit in their crowd. After our twenties, it happens less and less as we begin to believe in the character we created. And make no mistake, we have done the creating. While there are indeed some foundational traits that we are born with, we hone, perfect and re-enforce the attributes that match our beliefs abou our self-worth. For example, if our self-worth is low, an awkward social situation as a teen may cause us to label ourselves "shy." Instead of facing our fears, we lie to ourselves. As if we were born shy or something.

I looked up "shy." It means to be easily frightened or timid. This is not a personality trait embedded in your DNA. It is a decision that was made by you about your identity. You made a decision to put on the persona, the mask. If you are an adult who is "easily frightened or timid," what if you could be difficult to frighten and powerful? What would a difficult-to-frighten and powerful person do in a social situation? How would a difficult-to-frighten and powerful person handle an abusive person in their life? Would a difficult-to-frighten and powerful person allow toxic people around them or their family? How would such a person approach taking a risk on a business idea? Would they person get more respect from the people around them? If you struggle with confidence, try this little exercise. The next time you walk into a room, say in your mind, "You know me. I am difficult to frighten and powerful."

What character did you "sketch" during your formative years and then lock in by the end of your twenties? Think of some of your habits that are bad habits. Or think of areas where you keep failing. I want you to see that they are rooted in the character you "sketched." After I became aware that I was sabotaging my life, I began to wonder, is it possible that everyone is operating out of an identity that they are not even aware they have created? Could these identities be the roots of success or failure in our lives? Our very personalities hang in a frame of beliefs about who we are. Years and years of subconscious thoughts build the characters with which we so deeply identify. These characters come with strengths, weaknesses, and limitations that our brains make up based on our beliefs

49

about ourselves. If you can understand the truth, that you subconsciously decided what this character is capable of, then you can re-write this character's description to accomplish impossible things, genuinely impossible. Whatever you design, it will be so.

CHARACTER SKETCHING

People everywhere know how to character sketch.

"Well, you know me, I'm not bold and assertive in conversation."

"Well, you know me, I blather things out without thinking sometimes."

"Well, you know me, I'm always late."

"Well, you know me and my sweet tooth."

Do you see the game we play? Are you really content to continue role-playing in this manner? Can't you accept that you have simply created what the film industry calls a character sketch? A character sketch is a description of your character. The "shy guy." The "tough cookie." The "serious fellow." The reason you are not achieving your impossible life is that the character you created keeps sabotaging it. That's right. The character you sketched is not the type of character that would be cast for the upcoming fantasy piece you are writing. Is this making sense?

What I am talking about is being versus doing. Oh, and check this out. Did you know that in acting school, actors are taught to stop acting? Instead of learning how to act, they are taught how not to act and instead how to feel and channel emotion. They are taught how to be. I remember shooting a commercial where my character was supposed to be bored. I did take 1, and afterward, the director said, "Danny, don't act bored. You just are bored." The director could see me acting, which means I wasn't doing it right. I remember shooting that scene very well. I remember trying to perform the moves with my face that would make the audience say, "Oh look, he's bored." I wasn't bored. I was acting bored. I was doing the moves, but the director wanted me to embody the character. I needed to feel and become internally bored to sell the authenticity of this role.

"Acting is what's happening within you. It doesn't matter what's happening on your face."
-Helen Mirren

I stopped asking "What should I do?" and started asking, "Who do I want to be?" Doing differently helps only in a supplemental way, to achieve micro-goals along the way. Sure, we must take action. But I wanted to accomplish something impossible. I had to accept that I couldn't "do" it. Only dragons can breathe fire, and only children can be dragons.

WRITE YOUR LIFE

What character have you written for yourself to play? Are you the reclusive, mountain hermit? Are you the life of the party? Do you dive into rooms with an explosion or enter quietly? Are you the leader-type character, saving the day and keeping it all from falling apart? Are you the big gal who comes from a big family? Who is your character? We often write our character description based on what we believe the important people in our life expect. Some of their expectations are noble, but make sure you own them as well.

Not only are you the writer of this story, but you are also the main character. Not only did you come up with your life, but you are also starring in it. You are playing out the idea you have for yourself, and you believe that it's just happening in front of you! You are so good at acting that you think your life and circumstances are happening to you. The reality is that they are happening because of you. See the diff? This is the truth that leads to taking ownership.

I believed that I was responding to a predetermined life or circumstances. I thought that I was "making the best out of the cards I was dealt." Such are the slogans taught to me. My mentalities came with catchphrases that reinforced my beliefs. I didn't want to live in a universe with laws like "cause and effect." I wanted things to happen magically. The problem is that no matter what I believed, cause and effect were happening regardless. Reality didn't break its rules for my wrong beliefs. In fact, the effect of believing in destiny and magic was failure. I was a poor man on his deathbed, using the last of his strength to scratch off one more lotto ticket.

And yet every possible outcome lay before me all along, like something hidden in plain sight. I started believing loony ideas and began seeing things in the realm of potential, things beyond mere surviving on planet Earth. What if you could do this? What if you could see something breathtaking, something impossible?

DANNY THE CARPENTER

Once upon a time, I wrote a very fulfilling story called "Danny the carpenter." Danny (my character) was a humble man of modest means, but he loved what he did for a living. Although he could build many things, he got the most pleasure out of building furniture. Danny had a heated wood shop behind his house and took pride that he could include his kids in his work if he so desired. His humble work truck took him where he needed to go. Drinking coffee in his shop and enjoying the smell of cut wood, Danny thought to himself, This is who I am. I don't make much money, but I eat three meals a day and my family is healthy. God sure does take care of us. Danny believed that God gave him the life and reality he was experiencing.

But did God make phone calls to builders looking for work? Did God buy a tool belt and expensive tools? Did God put ads on Craigslist and in the newspaper? Was it God who did a great job and followed up with a professional invoice and a request for a referral? No, it was not. Hold on, hear me out a minute. Danny took action and did all those things. He took action according to his belief about his character—the romantic identity he had in being a carpenter. His character didn't go out and get a business degree and work at a bank. That would be out of character. Incongruent with his beliefs about what is important in life. Incongruent with what he wanted. Danny built a carpentry business, but more than that, he built a life experience. A reality. Carpentry happened because the character valued independence and family time.

Danny put on the mask or persona, the costume of the carpenter, and carried his personality in an appropriate manner that worked in the region in which he lived. He lived in the South. In the South, a door-holding, blue-collared gentleman who says "yes sir" and "ma'am" is a character that works. It's a character that he played so that he (me) could get to his (my) goals at the time. This was a great character and a great life. But I wanted something different. Something more. But this was the "real me."

How can I be something different? Something I'm not. What am I anyhow? What is the authentic me?

I've driven my share of broken-down trucks, but I remember when I got my first high-octane sports car. I'm just kidding, it was a Corolla. But that's not the fantasy I had in my head. I remember driving different, feeling different, and even dressing differently when I was a "Corolla Man." I didn't need an Italian, luxury sports car to feel like a powerful, successful businessman. I just needed a Corolla and an imagination.

THE AUTHENTIC YOU

What I'm saying is that the authentic you is simply the current character you are playing. You play this character because this character has worked for your past goals, or as they are often called, "dreams." Now you have new, impossible dreams. So what if you could simply write a new character description? What if you could dream up anything you want and this character would be that? Would it be worth learning new things and being clumsy again? How does this character's week look? What's going on in this character's home life? How would this new character dress? How much would this character weigh? Would this character's kids show them respect? Would this character be a photographer or play the violin or own a restaurant? Good people, this is precisely what you did to achieve your current reality. You just did it subconsciously!

The very things that you subconsciously dreamed about in the past are happening today. You're doing everything you set out to do! I don't mean that you are happy about it. I mean that you created it. I want you to do what I finally did: take ownership over your current situation. If you live in a van down by the river, it's because you took actions that led you there. You drove the van.

Something about the personality traits and habits of your character is bringing about your current results. It's not that you must start doing things differently. You must perform the much harder work, which is to start being different. It might feel like high treason to stop being what we call "ourselves." Our identity is so tied to our bad habits that it is painful to imagine them gone. We can get into self-abuse, where we tell ourselves that we are not good enough or strong enough. But remember, all you are now is the character you wrote years ago. It's your character that is weak, not you. I mean, what are you, anyhow? You are an amazing creature with superpowers, who can phase between the realms of potential and reality and create anything you envision. This is just your story so let's write in a new character now.

WRITE THE CHARACTER

In the past, you looked around your environment and designed a character that worked and got you by with minimal effort—though you may have worked very hard. Now, I want you to write a new character based on your great desire, not your environment. Don't write what is possible. Write what is not possible. Write something that will take a superhero to perform. Write something that normally would take a miracle to be real. Call it a fantasy. That's fine. Your dream character will build your dream life. Is your husband abusive toward you? Perhaps your new character has the ovaries to speak up and confront him. Maybe your new character is a powerful woman who respects herself and loves him too much to allow both of you to continue like this. This character will have to face fears and be brave and take risks and face danger. Go on, see what happens. A new adventure awaits. It may get harder before it gets better. So what? C'mon, unleash yourself on this world. Your family needs to see it, and you need to live it. What would it be like if you had a new sense of control over your future? What if the wind no longer blew you around the planet? What if you could be the wind?

Let's do exactly what is in our hearts to do today, to release all that we can be on this world. That's different for everybody. Our desires may change one week or five years from now, and that's ok. Do what you need to do, today. Before you write your new character (the one capable of achieving your impossibility), we need to take a hard look at your current character. What are your weaknesses? What do you keep failing at or are afraid to try? Does your character have a medical condition preventing you from achieving the impossible?

Doctor Norman Doidge wrote a book called The Brain That Changes Itself: Stories of personal Triumph from the Frontiers of Brain Science. This book discusses neuroplasticity and how the brain can rearrange itself and heal the body. He shares a story of a woman who was born with half a brain and how her brain rewired itself to function as a whole brain. This book is a fascinating read for anyone who feels trapped by the limitations of their body.

I'm not trying to tell you to do stuff, but it would be great if you did this next exercise. It's time to be very honest with yourself. Write the words on a piece of paper, "I can't because." Now, underneath that sentence, write down the reasons you are not able to do what you want to do. It will look something like this:

I can't because...
...I'm too old.
...I sleep in.
...I stay up too late.
...I'll lose what's important.
...I don't possess the skills.
...No one taught me how.
...I can't afford it.
...I don't even know how to begin.
...God doesn't want me to do this.

These are my real excuses. Your excuses may be similar, or write in your own. Take time, be thoughtful, and come up with some good ones. I want you to write some with real legitimacy. Like, "I can't because I don't have any arms or legs." Try to prove why you can't. There is a reason I want you to write these down. Something happens when we see our excuses in front of us. Suddenly, what used to be rock-solid proof of why we can't is now in the light. The covers have been ripped off! Suddenly they don't look so big or final, and we can deal with them one-by-one. So really try to prove it here. Once you have all your legitimate reasons written out, write an opposing, "What if I could?" statement underneath each one. So it should look something like this:

I'm too old.
But what if I could, even at my age? What would it look like if a person my age did this? How cool would it be if I were the FIRST person my age to do this?

No one taught me how.
But what if I could learn on my own? What would it be like if I had an extraordinary ability to self-learn?

I can't afford it.
But what if I could figure out a way to afford it? What would a person who could afford this do? What would my life look like if I could afford it?

This simple exercise will get your brain moving in a positive direction. Your new character won't have the hang-ups you used to have. Your new character will have new habits, strengths, and a new identity. Like a good actor, begin pretending and feeling the feelings that this character feels. With practice, you will move from pretending and into being. How does this new character respond to stress? With a level head and a skill for solving complex problems? Of course. How does this new character show love and vulnerability? Take time. You are the author. Write an original script. Go over your lines and practice your new role. Watch your family's shocked faces as they meet this new person. So go ahead, write your character who is capable, and start pretending.

Every morning, read your new character description with the intent of walking through your day as that new character. When decisions come up, or problems arise, ask yourself, "How would my new character handle this?" It won't be long before you start seeing massive results with this way of thinking. I want you to know that you are a masterful actor and that you can play any role you want.

Want a cool exercise to make this stick? Don't look into the mirror for three days. Each morning, read your character description and feel the new, powerful feelings that this new character has. I don't want you to look in the mirror, because I don't want the image you see to dictate who you are. Remember, who you are is who you decide to be, and it's not your body. On the fourth day, read your character description while looking in the mirror. Look yourself in the eyes and take yourself seriously. Don't blush or look away. Do this for three more days. As you look in the mirror, imagine that you are fusing this new idea with the image you see in the mirror.

Am I trying to brainwash you? Whatever. It's time to get weird and break out of your norm. Why? Because the character you created in the past is protecting you from the crisis that comes with failure, which means that it is protecting you from success. Being afraid is ok. Just be afraid and move forward! The identity that you think is so strong and in place is quite fragile. When you let go of the bold, "This is who I am" standard, you become free to be anything. Our old characters are protecting us from letting go and falling into the void. When we let go, we find that the pain that we feared doesn't hurt us, at least not in a real way.

03 WHAT IF YOU COULD?

We know for sure that if you are stressed, chemicals will release from your brain that harm your body. If you are relaxed, chemicals will release from your brain and heal your body. These chemicals are made of particles, and those particles are made of sub-atomic particles like quarks. If we were to zoom in and look at anything at the smallest level, we would see a collection of tiny things, bonded together in different ways. When we see anything, we see an assembled collection of atoms and other building blocks. If you zoomed into your eye, you would cease to see an "eye." You would see an entire galaxy of particles, moving about as if propelled by an unseen power. These particles seem to have a will, undisclosed to you. Injure yourself, and particles spring into action and begin making their way to their repair assignment. They are like angels, constrained to do the will of their creator. These actions take place at the quantum level, and it's incredible.

This is the space where things change based on your thoughts and desires. Brain thought isn't just an idea in your head. Physical things happen, and connections are made. Complex pathways from one part of the brain to another are formed. Crazier still, these pathways also extend to the heart and vice versa. Modern people put so much emphasis on the mind as our conscious thought-organ, but there are so many new studies demonstrating the thought signals that the heart sends to the mind. We even have neurons (communication networks made of cells) in our hearts and throughout our bodies. We've known for decades, for example, that stress leads to heart attacks. The heart and gut talk to the mind as well as listen to it.

So a self-limiting belief can ruin your life, biologically speaking. Simply doubt that you can do a thing, and your brain's electrical system goes nuts firing information on a complex highway of axons, synapses, cells and neurons. Atoms begin fusing. Chemical bonds form signals that you perceive as thoughts and emotions. These activities, thoughts and emotions make their way through the data channels of your muscular system and out to your frowning face! You then take faux action and, of course, fail, proving your self-fulfilling prophecy to yourself.

Zoom in to the fundamental levels of the building blocks that make up "you," and we find pure, creative energy—the power to wreck your life or to do the impossible. We're not talking ideas here. We're talking measurable reality. So it's not "mind over matter." The mind is matter. When you tap into your limitless power, reality itself will bend to your will. I'm going further. You are not even subject to the laws of reality. Why? Because reality is totally subjective. Reality means what we know of as real today. Scientifically speaking, that changes daily. Humans decide what is possible and what is not. Every day we see more profound and deeper possibilities.

THE 4 MINUTE MILE

What once was impossible and not realistic is now standard. In the mid-1950s, humanity believed that a mile could not be run in under four minutes. We thought that our hearts would explode and we would die. Distance runner John Landy ran a mile in four minutes and two seconds several times. He is on record saying this: "Frankly, I think the four-minute mile is beyond my capabilities. Two seconds may not sound much, but to me, it's like trying to break through a brick wall. Someone may achieve the four-minute mile the world is wanting so desperately, but I don't think I can."

Do you know what happened next? A man named Roger Bannister ran the mile in 3:59.4. He broke humanity's mental barrier (not a physical barrier) by a little over half a second! Then, amazingly, just forty-six days later, John Landy ran a mile in 3:57.9! What?! This is the man who just said that the four-minute mile was "beyond [his] capabilities." And so it was! What changed? Roger Bannister's action sent shockwaves throughout the belief system of humanity. The news of his accomplishment rewired thousands of athletes' brains and gave them superpowers!

They had a new power to do the impossible. Since then, scores of people have run the four-minute mile. What was once fantasy is now a reality, wrought from the realm of potential! It is now an actuality. Henry Ford famously said, "Whether you think you can, or you think you can't—you're right." When I look throughout history at the people who have accomplished great things, I see one, simple golden thread in common. They believed they could!

Muhammed Ali said, "I said I was the greatest before I knew I was." Similarly, professional basketball players are trained to visualize the ball going into the basket.

Boxers who "trash talk" before the fight often win because they get into their opponent's head while simultaneously pumping themselves up. They know that if they can scare the enemy, they can win. When a fighter believes that they are weaker, they are.

So what are the desires of your heart? Not everyone wants to be a basketball player. Not everyone wants to open a restaurant. What's the thing you want? Do you sorta want to lose weight? Do you sorta want to start a business? Do you sorta want to be free from drugs? Do you sorta want whatever it is you want? If that's you, then let me give you a promise right now. You won't do it. But if you want this secret thing of yours with all of your heart and all of your soul and all of your mind, you will get it. Right now, say out loud the thing you want with all of your heart, soul and mind. Now let me ask you a question. Do you want it with all of your strength? With all of your action, I mean. What actions are backing up your purported desires? Desire without work is dead.

With that in mind, let's talk about the four parts of us. By consciously directing these four parts, you will get in touch with the kind of person you really want to show up as on this planet, doing whatever flows from this new space you have created.

WITH ALL YOUR HEART

Did you know that your heart has neurons? A neuron is an electrically excitable cell that receives, processes and transmits information through electrical and chemical signals. These are the vehicles that carry impulses and thoughts around the brain and, as we are now learning, around the heart and body. Wow! Could the heart be an "intelligent" organ? Could it have a will? Could it compel you to do things? I don't believe that your consciousness is trapped in your brain or any part of your body. I do, however, believe that your consciousness acts out or flows onto this planet via your body. And the way it does that biologically is via the nervous system. Your true eternal state, blasting through your body, causing neurons and cells to light up and change. That's the picture I have in my mind.

When we speak of doing something with all of our heart, what do we mean by that? We mean with all of our feeling, emotion and passion. When we tell someone to do something with all of their heart, we mean we want them to genuinely feel what it is they are doing and to do it with gumption and ownership. If a loved one dies, we don't keep them in our minds, we hold them in our hearts—our special place of abundant love and sacrifice. Your heart is a powerful place, but for all its power, it has a great weakness. It can get wounded and hurt in ways that affect all of your life. Has your heart ever hurt? I'll bet you can remember the first time your heart was damaged. It probably hurts now to think about it. That's because your brain didn't get hurt, your heart did—the seat of emotion and vulnerability. It's possible for your heart to hurt bad enough that it just quits. Many heart attacks happen after the death of a loved one. Doctors say that the grief and stresses placed on the heart activate the "fight or flight" response. This increases heart rate and blood pressure, which cuts off blood flow and can result in a heart attack. You can truly die of a broken heart.

But what if you could harness the power of the heart? I believe exercise is a great way to begin this process. I just started running. I'll be honest. It was painful the first four times I ran. On run number six, however, something changed. It was as if I was outside of my body, distant in thought. After about ten minutes of running, I had a breakthrough, and I no longer felt the groan of my body. I wasn't thinking about being out of breath or how hard my heart was beating. I was thinking about how we are creators. I felt as if I wasn't just running down the road, but striding toward my goals. The run itself felt like movement toward my dreams. I began saying, out loud, what it was I wanted with all my heart. When I got home, I went into my office and locked the door.

Immediately, I sat down and meditated on those desires. I pictured myself attaining my goal, and as I did, I began feeling serious and passionate about the journey to get there. Something was happening in my heart. My motivation soared. I wanted to perform a celebratory toe touch (everyone does those, right?), and begin working immediately. I didn't know it at the time, but I was harnessing the power of my heart. I think it's important to understand what we want with all of our heart. When our heart is in the right place, we move forward with passion and attain what we are after.

Exercise isn't the thing in and of itself. Instead, it is just a powerful tool in your belt. You can use it to rev the body systems and get them flowing. This provides clarity of thought and allows you to get in touch with what you want, or as some call it, listening to your heart! When we can consciously understand what our heart desires, we can move forward with great passion and direction.

WITH ALL YOUR SOUL

I have read many, many, many fascinating ideas about the soul. Some believe that the soul is just an idea or description of our thinking mind. Others believe it's an actual thing or consciousness trapped inside our body, causing it to have life. I'm no guru, and I'll admit that I don't have a special expertise on this subject, but I don't believe anyone does. You can't exactly get a soul out and look at it. Many have come to very compelling personal beliefs about the soul, but they are just that—personal beliefs. That is because I believe the soul can only be observed by senses outside of the five primary senses of the body. Or rather, the soul could be the eternal being doing the observing, the eye of eternity. See what I mean? The discussion of a soul, one that regards the soul as a real thing, cannot be founded on current scientific understanding. (The sci-fi lover in me is quite comfortable with that. Many of today's technologies were yesterday's science fiction fantasies.) Rather, it must be discussed based on the harmony of personal and global experience, both ancient and modern. All we have is what we have discussed and experienced throughout history, and such a discussion should be fresh and ongoing. All of the written knowledge is available to anyone who has an internet connection. Your personal experience, however, is where it matters. That is where you gain an awareness of the you that sees through your eyes. The you that is not a slave to your body or circumstances. The you that is, dare I say, elsewhere, perhaps sitting in a heavenly place. You must admit, something not the eye sees through these eyes of ours! The eyes are windows. They cannot be us. But I can't prove this using the senses of the body.

And so, I write the following disclaimer.

The following musings on the soul are neither concrete nor provable. The author acknowledges that such lofty things are scantily understood and even more pitifully explained. Though attempts at explaining portions of the invisible world will be made, they are offered with the understanding that the author merely possesses the language and understanding of humans and thus, such explanations will, in the end, be insufficient.

And yet, we must talk about the soul, as I was required to go after my impossible life with all of it, with all of my soul. It all begins in the soul. I will classify the soul as the part of us that controls and directs the body: a person's free spirit and not their personality. In other words, you might be timid. But your soul is not. "Timid" describes your learned behavior from your environment. Like a professional actor, you "act" timid. Being timid is an attempt to protect yourself. Now, through frequent use, it has become part of your personality. But when we look into the "soul" of who you are, we don't find timidity. Who are you if we aren't looking at your body or your personality? Or do you believe that you are body + personality? Is it hard to accept that there is an invisible you?

My soul was a stranger. I walked the earth and made decisions without purpose or end. I lived to survive. I was out of touch with the soul of who I was. It's like my system was on autopilot and I, the pilot, was asleep.

GETTING SPOOKY

Hold on. Does this make you nervous? I get it. We didn't have trusted people in our lives teach this to us. Modern thought and society itself scream against it.

This is why I was afraid—holding still and getting in touch with deeper things. Dare we, modern people, call this "prayer?" Oh, I know it's out of fashion, but I think it's worth your consideration. At first, I would come to these prayer sessions very busy-minded and spirited, saying all sorts of wishes or talking out my fears, as if I knew what should be done. As time progressed, I became more focused. I would bring one major issue before the "council," if I could describe it that way. I don't know. That's the way it felt. It felt like I was bringing the major things of life before a team of powerful counselors and they helped me sort it all. I usually leave these sessions knowing what to do. Dare we, modern people call this council, "God?" So yeah, I began to bring one major issue at a time to the council. I would picture myself writing the item down on a piece of paper and then sliding it over to the council. Sometimes I would actually write my problems on paper, slide it over, and look up for an answer. Call me weird, I don't care. I would often leave these sessions with an obvious solution, or one would come to me later that week. Could people be right when they say that "God answers prayer?"

UNEXPECTED COOLNESS

There was another amazing thing happening in these sessions. As I got into the rhythm of these moments, I began coming less and less with needs. I was becoming the person who already knew what to do. I was becoming the right person for the job. I can now come to these sessions for any need at all. If I need to blather out my rants, then fine, or if I need one solid answer, it's there for me too. Mostly now, though, I can just come and bask in a glorious doing of nothing, a trust that someone greater than myself is with me, blowing wind in my sails.

Modern friends, you don't have to be afraid of this. Try and do this for just five minutes the first time. Then do ten. If you feel you can't build a ten-minute break into your day, it's a sure sign that you should.

The more time I spent in prayer, the more clear my mind became. Surely this soul thing must be real! It must be a part of us, as much as our heart and mind. It must be the invisible us, the part of us that connects with God. Your heart will begin to feel limitless as you listen to your soul. The soul is unrestricted by time and free to move in any direction. It's free to create anything you want and achieve any goal. Excuses will melt away, and direction will become abundantly clear. You will find yourself living your fantasies, and you will call it your life.

It's exciting to me that we barely understand anything. We only have glimpses of understanding. At this infant stage of human history, even our most celebrated scientists will tell you that what we don't know is infinitely greater than what we do. Humans are finally treating the heart and soul with the same level of fascination and study as we have the mind. We want to awaken the powerful soul and let it direct the heart, the mind, and the actions you take. This, I believe, is the miracle God gives us: the gift of life. It's the gift of awakening to our eternal self. When we awaken the soul, we understand that we are limitless. When truly owned, the belief of our limitlessness will strip excuses and ignite the power to accomplish the impossible thing. Your soul, the real you, is without boundary. Believe that your soul is real; this is important.

Your soul doesn't experience pain. It cannot suffer loss or harm in any way. It doesn't see risk as a serious matter but rather a fun world in which to play. It fears nothing. It fears nothing. It fears nothing. Your soul is the explorer, on its journey through the earth. It does not waver between opinions nor shy away from the wild path. It looks at you now with fierce expectation. Will you seek what you desire, with all of your soul?

Are you mentally focused? Are you strong of mind? Luckily, our fabulous brains have built-in warning indicators, letting us know when our minds are weak. Arguing, striving and stress are signs that we need to get our minds right. We think we are mad about traffic or our kids or other people, but in reality, we are frustrated about deeper things. However, when our minds are clear about what we want, we set it to achieve our goals with decided purpose. The results are beautiful. Our frustrations diminish (road rage, strife, etc.), and we are filled with peace. A peaceful mind is the hallmark of a strong mind.

My cool friend Pearl told me about a cool study from The Ohio State University, linking marital stress with gut-health issues. Couples that argue using demeaning phrases and criticism can suffer from more frequent health problems. Stress from hostile relationships can cause leaky gut, a condition in which undigested food and bacteria leach into the bloodstream. Leaky gut creates a mountain of health and emotional problems, like depression. Wait, did leaky gut cause these issues, or did the couples who demean each other cause them? Your mind can harm your body and destroy your life.

In our hearts, our seats of desire, we emotionally make decisions about what we want. Then we must pass the torch to the mind. If the heart is where we dream, then the mind is where we plan and strategize those dreams. Computation and logic is the territory of the mind. It is the mission control center, giving commands to the body for all that the body will accomplish on the earth. I often see the mind as our biocomputer. But what if the mind is being unreasonable? What if the neurons were firing down well-trod yet harmful and defeating pathways. What if they were firing incorrectly and causing you to come to the wrong conclusions? Would you know that your perspective was incorrect? Of course not! Folly is concealed from its host.

You would, of course, inevitably make the wrong decisions in your life. You would not succeed at the things you wanted most. Though your tongue would claim it wanted success, you would not behave in a way that brought it about. This is called self-sabotage. It is the final stage of not being right, the subconscious ruining of your success. Don't say, "Well, things just didn't work out." Things don't ever work out. You must work them out. But this is what happens when you don't harness your mind. You will be the subject of well-founded yet incorrect conclusions and reasoning. Telling the body to do this and that until "fate," as you will call it, ruins your success and pulls you to the grave.

HARNESS THE MIND

The thing about being wrong is that you never know you are. In Memphis, we would say, "You best get yo mind right!" So how do we harness the mind? Sometimes, our mind wants to be weak and wander. I found a straightforward tool for keeping my mind on track—a business plan. I learned that successful people write business plans. They state their end goal and design a master plan to get there. Then they execute their project in a timely manner. This is why they achieve success over and over. A business plan is a conscious strategy for bringing what you desire to pass. It helps you take ownership over who you want to be and what you can accomplish. What if it was not just for others but you? A business plan is just an accountability tool to keep your goals in check. Even if you've never made a business plan, you can do it. Let's make a simple, tiny plan, mmk? Write down the thing you want to accomplish. Underneath that, write down the action steps needed to get what you want. You might not know the action step, but pick up a pencil and hover it over a page until it comes out. Believe that it's in you. You can get as elaborate or specific as you want here, but don't overcomplicate it. Read your plan every week and take action on the work you must do to get what you want. That's all it takes. I want to encourage you to make up your mind right now. Listen to your soul, your most powerful self, the you from the future who is telling you that it's worth it. Come to a firm conclusion to make a plan and pursue your desire with all of your mind, right now.

WITH ALL YOUR STRENGTH

Now that a plan has been made with the mind, it's time to execute this plan with all of your strength. With all of your human engine, move forward. Email the right people, make strategic phone calls, go to a gym, meet new people, get on a solid plan for how you eat. Take action! And take that action with all of your strength. Go to bed on time and exhausted. Wake up early and scream. Whatever it takes. People who have done great things on the Earth, hands down, have always been people of action. From every part of the world, men, women and children have shaken nations with their actions. A person who believes and takes action will stagger the world with what they can do. These are the mountain-tamers. They have wisdom to navigate the high places of the earth, and they see the desires of their hearts come to pass. They are an example to their children and their entire family tree from that point in history forward. Truly, this is how history is made.

When you do something with all of your strength, it means to do it with all of your actions. Desire without work is for people who believe in destiny. Think about that. Every forward action you take increases potential and possibilities in your life. Your mind expands its horizons as to what is even possible in the first place. Those new possibilities give birth to more questions. You begin to test limitations and find that many of them you created in your mind. That, of course, inspires riskier action, and the whole thing compounds and grows exponentially. This bouncing back and forth of beliefs, which inspire actions, which create new beliefs, which inspire bigger actions, is atomic. Strategy and execution, consistently over time, is how passionate people achieve impossibilities. You yourself, not fate, will pull it from the realm of potential.

WITH ALL OF YOU

Be honest with yourself. Have you done the work to engage the entire you? Have you aimed your entire self at the thing you want most, bringing all of your powers to the endeavor? Have you made up your mind to take action, with all of your heart and soul? Do you passionately work at it with all your:

1. Heart (emotions and vulnerability)
2. Soul (seeing yourself eternal, limitless, powerful and timeless)
3. Mind (writing down a plan)
4. Strength (bold, consistent action)

Or are you content to let this stay a dream, something for others but not you? Today, make up your mind to take action, with all of your heart and soul.

My favorite movies are the ones that aren't explained but left up to the audience to interpret. Take the movie Inception, directed by Christopher Nolan and starring Leonardo DiCaprio. In this movie, the characters are able to enter other people's dreams and even extract valuable information from those people. Entering the dream world seems very real, and the characters have a difficult time distinguishing the dream world from reality. Leonardo's character "Cobb" has a metal spinning top in his pocket. The purpose of this top is to help him figure out whether he is in the dream world or in the real world. To figure this out, he spins the top. If the top spins perpetually, he knows that he can't be in the real world, as "real" spinning tops eventually slow down and stop spinning. If the top spins normally but then slows down and stops, then Cobb knows he's in the real world.

Cobb's been framed for a serious crime, and he has to go into hiding, away from his children. His one desire is to be with his children again. In the closing scene, Cobb is finally reunited with his children but isn't sure if it is real or if he is in a dream. Desperate to find out the truth, he spins his metal top. The camera zooms in while the top spins on a table, but before we get a chance to see whether it spins perpetually or falls as it should, we cut to the credits! Was he finally with his kids or was he in a dream?

In an interview, Leonardo DiCaprio said that he chooses to believe that the top fell and that Cobb was with his children again. Who is to argue with that? You, the observer, get to apply the meaning. Whatever you think it means, it does.

Whatever you believe about the world, it's true. At least for you. Whatever is in your head is reality. Have you ever heard anyone say: "What I currently believe is wrong." Go ahead, make a list of all the wrong things you believe.

Strange, right? Everything you believe is "right." Sure, of course it is.

Whatever you believe about yourself, you are right. Everything in your life will be a proclamation to what you believe about yourself. Your weight, job, hobbies, and even friend choices are all a reflection of the invisible you—the you that no one can see. The more aware you become of the unseen you, the less you will be an unreasonable creature of habit and impulse. You can navigate the world with limitless possibility because you will design what is real. You really are the designer of your reality.

Think about it—everything you see in your life right now, you created. Or perhaps you think that God designed the good things and the devil designed the bad? Where does that leave you? It leaves you powerless. Powerlessness is a subtle depression often medicated with "God's will" or "fate." But what if you accepted responsibility for the current design of your life? What if you relished in the beautiful things you made and grieved the ugly stuff? What if you took ownership of the script you wrote and the resulting play? And what if you could re-write the whole thing? What if your wildest, most impossible desires could come to pass because you willed it so?

05 **WHAT ARE YOU WORTH?**

"Ultimately, we are not the avatars we create. We are not the image on the film stock; we're the light that shines through"

-Jim Carrey

What is the value of you? Inside our minds, we have an estimation of our price. Are you worth one million dollars? Are you worth less than that? Are you worthless than that? Are you worthless? Are you? Are you worth more than that? How much more? Can you put a number on it? Are you priceless? Is your price without end? If you had to think of a number, what would it be?

I know, when we try to measure ourselves using numbers, it just gets silly. We can't do it. We have another measurement system, our feelings. Many men don't want to hear it, but they are just as epically emotional as women. All humans are emotional. We all weigh ourselves and create things around us according to what we esteem. Counselors, for example, will talk with abused adults about their worth. When we value ourselves correctly, we will not allow abuse in our life. Not from others, or in the form of self-abuse or self-sabotage. You, like I was, might not even be aware of a worth issue in your life. But if you are consistently failing or having low life experiences, it's worth discussing the feelings that subconsciously accompany your pictures of success.

No one pictures the thing they want and then consciously says, "I'm not worth that." Instead, we feel fear or that we shouldn't do it. Maybe our family doesn't want us to, or maybe even God is against it—how horrifying. Worthless people shouldn't have an amazing husband or a fantastic career. Worthless people say things when they fail like, "Of course, story of my life." Little phrases like that might not seem like much, but they are revealing. Is failure the story of your life? Who is writing this terrible story?

OUR INNER STATE

For your mind to release impossibility onto the earth, your internal system needs a significant self-worth upgrade. If you believe that you aren't worth your desires coming to pass, then you will never create them in your life. Our minds and hearts can be harmed. That affects us at a cellular level and breaks down our bodies. We have gut issues, and we have headaches; we have sickness and death. Any time you feel frustration or pain in your heart or your life, it is your body's way of telling you that you need to either change things or adjust your perspective. Your perspective is a light in your life. If your perspective is healthy, everything in your life will be full of brilliant, beautiful light. But if your perspective and outlook—your "internal state"— is unhealthy, your whole life will be unhealthy. Look at a person whose inner state is unhealthy. Everything in their life is jacked. It all brings them frustration and disappointment—unhappiness. But you are an eternal creature with superpowers.

In you is a limitless power to change your world. Your home, work, external relationships and family are your world. Here, all your fields can grow green and be drenched with flowers and sunshine. But it's not about doing things differently. It's about being internally different. You must grow and change. You must heal. We're not waiting on the world to change. The world is waiting for us. Take action now! Don't lie around groaning. Maya Angelou famously said, "If you don't like something, change it. If you can't change it, change your attitude."

Outside of abuses you can't control, misery is a self-inflicted wound. Ninety-nine percent of all our problems come from unconscious low self-worth. I say unconscious because nobody is walking around talking about or even aware of their low self-worth. It just manifests in every area of their life. But we can't change "they." We need to focus on the inner us.

SELF LOVE

I was so frustrated with people all the time. "Don't they know how much I love them?" I would ask myself internally. "How can they not show me the same love and dedication I show them?" When I was in that state, my so-called love for them was just a projection of what I wanted from them. My kind acts and gifts to them were merely an attempt to teach them how to love me. And when it didn't happen in return? Hurt! Misunderstandings! My "love" for them was an attempt to feel love from them. Does that make sense? The more empty we are, the worse this is... and the inevitable happens: blame. "It's my mother's fault, you know. If she weren't so _____ we could all be happy." Or, "When will my spouse stop _____? I'll never be complete until they do." Sad soul! Do your mother and spouse hold the keys to your peace and happiness? No, they don't.

If things go bad for you
And make you a bit ashamed
Often you will find out that
You have yourself to blame
Swiftly we ran to mischief
And then the bad luck came
Why do we fault others?
We have ourselves to blame
Whatever happens to us,
Here is what we say
"Had it not been for so-and-so
Things wouldn't have gone that way."
And if you are short of friends,
I'll tell you what to do
Make an examination,
You'll find the faults in you.

You're the captain of your ship,
So agree with the same
If you travel downward
You have yourself to blame
-Mayme White Miller

Have you ever heard the phrase, "If you can't love yourself, you can't love others." I used to disagree with that. I thought self-love was prideful and selfish. I was wrong. If you are full of love, you will spill over. Everyone and everything around you will bloom and grow like a well-watered garden. It will almost be impossible to hurt and offend you. It will be almost impossible to hurt and offend you. It will be almost impossible to hurt and offend you. Catch that? You will bring life to your world. If, however, your heart is empty, you will continuously search for validation outside of yourself. And whoever withholds said validation will get all of your blame. You will believe that they are the source of your problem. So let's get our validation from an internal source rather than an external source. How many children go to school every day hoping to have their classmates answer questions about whether they are beautiful, valid, enough? If they don't get validation in class, perhaps they'll get it on social media. How many children turn into adults still with question marks on their foreheads?

Am I valuable?
What is my worth?
Does the love I give matter?
Do I have what it takes?

There is a you, deep inside, that wants to love yourself. The you that loves yourself might be a total stranger right now. You might have to meet this person for the first time. Am I getting touchy-feely? Scary, I know. This type of vulnerability can be one of the hardest things we'll do. Is this new person calmer? More in control when making hard decisions? How does the you that you love treat their body? Sacred. C'mon and parent yourself. Maybe no one has ever nurtured you, but that doesn't matter anymore. What would you want for your child to believe about themselves? It's time to believe those beautiful things about you.

2 QUEENS

Queen Sally decides to take a stroll through her kingdom. As she walks down the streets, not one person makes eye contact or even looks up to acknowledge her presence. "They all hate me," she thinks. "They can't even look up for a second to show their queen the respect she deserves.

They don't love me, and I'll never walk through town again."

Meanwhile, in another kingdom, Queen Mary decides to take a stroll through her town as well. As she walks down the streets, not one person makes eye contact or even looks up to acknowledge her presence either. "Oh my, she thinks, they have so much love and respect for me that they won't even look in my direction. It's ok, people! I am a good queen, and you don't have to be afraid." She concludes, "I must walk through this town every day until these wonderful people know beyond a shadow of a doubt my love for them."

Let me ask you, which queen was right? Queen Sally or Queen Mary? They both are. As a queen thinks in her heart, so she is. Whatever perspective is in her mind is her reality. Who is to argue that their reality is wrong? Both queens will live a life based on their conclusions about what their experiences mean, and everything in their kingdom will reflect their perspective. Her children, her husband, her body, her house—all manifestations of the inner state of the queen. All self-fulfilling prophecies, fulfilled by a queen with either a full or empty heart. The wise queen doesn't walk through town with a big question mark on her forehead. Events and people don't define you or design your life. You are the captain of your ship. Don't look for a sign in the clouds; your direction comes from your heart. Queen Sally was a blamer. Queen Mary took ownership. Ownership is scary, and many people are afraid of it.

I want you to have power over the aspects of your personality that your false interpretations of your past have sculpted. Then your mind won't be limited by your past, and your value of yourself will increase. Moving forward in boldness has everything to do with your self-worth.

81

In this book, my main case is that you can create anything in your life. If, however, your self-worth is jacked, then you will go about sabotaging the whole thing. You will do this to prove to yourself that you are not strong or capable enough. It's easier than trying. Less painful than failing. So we self-fulfill our prophecies according to our self-worth. If our self-worth is low, we will create low-level things in our life. Those things will disappoint us, but at least they won't scare us. They have been designed to disappoint, by you.

Yes, own it. We will subconsciously create failures to confirm our root beliefs about ourselves. We want the outside to match the inside. We will lie to ourselves that circumstances just turned out that way, but in reality, we were the orchestrator of the thing. We wanted it that way. We surround ourselves with a world that matches the inside of our hearts. Everything in your world around you is an expression of you. An illustration of your fears or your love. You are in constant creation. Constantly planting. Constantly watering. Whether you mean to or not, you are always making things happen. I hope you will begin doing this consciously. I hope you will start designing the things that you want to happen and bring them about with great assurance and power, in a way that soberly and consistently brings what you want into reality. May you be known for this new unique ability to make things happen.

(Side note. I want to make room for special circumstances. Some things in your world may not have been created by you. For example, you might be reading this as a fifteen-year-old, and you are living in a broken home that you DID NOT create. That's not what I mean. If that is you, don't take ownership of creating that. Instead, begin taking ownership of your future and what you can control. A child in an abusive home will face many lions. Don't be afraid.)

Empowering self-worth is scary and risky. If our self-worth is high, we will surround ourselves with good and beautiful people and experiences. We will create beauty all around us and bring healing to our world while we laugh. Something happens when we truly, in our heart of hearts, believe that we can pull this thing off. Because when we believe the reality that we can, we suddenly realize that if we don't, it is because we chose not to. And that is called ownership. It's finally fessing up that you are not living your wild, impossible life, and that the reason you aren't is because you don't want to. It's acknowledging that you are quite content to be frustrated and disappointed rather than put the work in and risk your carefully crafted identity. Some are even ready to die rather than perform this deep, internal work. I think you have to decide if you believe in destiny or creation. Believing in destiny is way more comfortable than believing that you have the power of creation. Once you believe that you can create what you want, you'll do it.

TIME TRAVEL

Want to travel back in time? Change your perspective. Want to change the future? Take action. Before my "I'll do it" breakthrough, everything in my past was crap. My view was that I went from one unfortunate event to the next. I saw my childhood as misfortunes happening to me over and over, and I had nothing to guide me out of it. All of this meant that I was destined to be a loser. And so I was a big, freaking loser. I saw my life as an abysmal failure. I was a deplorable super-loser. But what if I could go back in time and change my history? I don't mean change what happened. We've all seen what happens in the movies when you change history! Instead, what if I could go back and witness the events as an observer rather than a participant. What if I could re-write what everything meant?

I closed my eyes, went back to events in my mind, and chose to see them from a higher perspective. I took with me a pen and paper, and I wrote a powerful narrative about the person I was watching and the amazing things in store for him. I wrote new meanings to events in the past. I made them happen for me rather than to me. I created a person who was able to use pain and loss for great good—what a superpower. Of course, time travel is real. If one can time travel like that, how much more real does it get? It would be less amazing to be able to physically time travel yet not able to re-write history. If the past is affecting your present negatively, then it's not the past, is it? It's the now. The past isn't in the realm of the actual. It exists only in your mind. So what happened in the past is up to you. You are the master of time.

For example, I had no family identity, but that taught me the things I wrote in the "character-sketching" section. I learned that identity is a made-up thing anyway, and we can write whatever we want for our character. I technically grew up in a broken home, and so no one taught me how to be. No template to reference. Did I need the crazy childhood to be where I am today? Most likely yes, but I don't know how everything works. All I know is what I can control, and that is my perspective. Having a dark perspective leads to a very specific outcome: darkness. But if my perspective is amazing, powerful and at times full-on fantasy, then what is my reality? What is the reality in which I choose to live? I choose to live in a fantastic reality. Where else should I flipping live?

Regret is like a dark, cold and cracked spot in your heart. It affects how you see things today. It's a way of looking back on yourself with disgust. Regret is the rod you beat yourself with, seeking justice for your failures. It is a hiding place for low self-worth, and it is holding you back.

SELF LIMITING BELIEFS

Self-limiting beliefs, when watered with wrong thoughts, grow into a permanent part of a person's personality and reality. Remember, the word personality comes from the Latin "persona," and it means a mask or character in a play. It's not something we are born with but rather something we put on in accordance with what we identify with as we grow up. So from self-limiting beliefs grows a negative reality, which happens when we take action on our wrong beliefs and bring them into the real world. Before you know it, you'll believe your own belief! "Well you know, after all, I've always been that way," you say. Then, believing that you've always been "that way," you begin to act "that way." Thus proving to yourself and the world that you've always been "that way." It's easier to be "that way" than change, isn't it? And so now you're the weak guy, the fat girl, the loser, the failure who can't. Well, it's time to be brave. You can redesign a new system at any age. You can stop being "that way" anytime you like.

What's your self-limiting belief? Write it down if necessary. Either something happened, or something was said that made you believe this. Perhaps you were walking through your kitchen as a teenager and heard your mom saying to your uncle on the phone, "Ya know Frank, obesity runs in the family." Years later, you learn from cousin Milda that Aunt Darcy can't make the family reunion this year due to heart surgery. "After all," Milda says, "obesity runs in the family." Five years later you look in the mirror and see yourself starting to look a little like Uncle Frank. After all, the voice in your head says, obesity runs in the family. Do you know what actually runs in the family? Self-limiting beliefs!

YOUR UNIQUE ABILITY

Self-limiting beliefs must go, because they keep our worth low. Like little guards, making sure you don't step out of the pre-arranged system. The system you call "you." This entire book is an attempt to tear down the construct you built called "you." Why? Because most likely you are reading this because you are not getting the results you want out of some aspect of your life. The reason you are not getting those results is that you are being a certain way (as opposed to doing the wrong things). The reason you are being the wrong way is that you believe the wrong conclusions about your experiences and ultimately your worth to the world. So if you don't identify with a limitless, powerful creature who can create anything you want, reframe yourself to see your great worth. Then you will lose weight, get a promotion, start a business, or succeed at whatever it is you want to do. Why? Because failure is not congruent with your new, powerful beliefs. You are not linked to the kind of creature that fails. You have a unique ability to get anything you want. You're an "I'll do it" person. Overcoming self-limitation is massive and can be scary. I can tell you from experience. It's worth the fight.

ACHIEVE ESCAPE VELOCITY

It's pretty easy nowadays to fly around the Earth. I personally know people who have their pilot's licenses.

They simply rent planes from time to time and zoom around wherever they want to go. But what if you wanted to go beyond Earth and travel to the great beyond? Space travel requires something that is currently very hard to safely achieve. It's called "escape velocity." The escape velocity from Earth is about 25,020 miles per hour—how fast you need to travel in order to break through the Earth's atmosphere.

If you want to fly around like everybody else, then just go copy them. However, I imagine you are reading this book because you want to go higher. If you want to go interstellar, then you need to achieve escape velocity! You can't fly like everybody else. You need the right kind of ship. You need to reach impossible speeds to go to impossible places.

My hunch is that the thing you want the most is going to require a massive breakthrough. That breakthrough won't happen accidentally. It will require all of you and more. Don't worry, you can do this, and I want to help make it simple. So let's summarize the three action steps in this book for achieving escape velocity in your life and making impossibilities happen.

A.E.V. ACHIEVE ESCAPE VELOCITY

1. Achieve. Re-write your capable character.
We are talking about being vs doing. Don't just do things differently. Write down the description of the new, powerful character who doesn't make excuses and knows exactly how to break through anything. Whenever the words "I can't" form in your head, ask the question, "But what if I could?" What does this character eat? What does this character wear? Become this person, make it the authentic you, and let others deal with it. You may feel like you're playing dress-up at first. Get over it.

2. Escape. Make a business plan.

Escape the gravitational pull of failure by making a plan. Write down the impossible thing that must be done and create the steps needed to get there. You no longer don't know how. You are the kind of person who can come up with a road map. You are so good at this that you will be able to help others as well.

3. Velocity. Take action.

Begin the work today. Don't wait on the right timing or season. Recognize waiting as a hiding place for fear. Aim your entire self (heart, soul, mind and strength) at what you desire.
#wiyc

CHILDHOOD

What if you could? This is the question of a child. When I was young, I did this with my friends. "What if I could turn into a creature with a special power to jump as high as buildings?" I would ask my neighborhood friend. Or, "What if I could fly anywhere I wanted?" I remember, all I've ever wanted to do is fly and breath underwater. I still have dreams at night that I have these abilities. Maybe one day I will. What are these crazy desires, really? I think it's the desire for limitlessness, to be unencumbered by restriction. I want to fly because I want to be free to go anywhere and do anything. I want to explore the high places of Earth. I also wish I could breathe underwater because I want to explore the depths as well. With those two abilities, no place would be impossible to access. But I'm just imposing the idea of going anywhere and doing anything into my dreams at night. What I really want is to awaken in the day and be limitless in my relationships, in my career, in my goals, in what I create and bring to the world. That's what WIYC is all about. It's about being a child again. It's the question that will change everything.

My daughter came running into the room the other day and said, "Daddy, look, I'm a dragon!" Her arms were spread wide out beside her. Clearly they were dragon wings! Wait, did she mean she was acting like a dragon? But that's not what she said. She said, I am a dragon. Do you see the power that children have? It's the power we lost, the power to do and be anything we want. Who were you as a child? What did you want as a child? What did you give up because the adults told you that you must? Awaken the child!

What if you could be a child again? What if you could reclaim your power of creation? Children don't pursue their dreams, they create the fantasy around them. They are, without effort, in touch with their gift of creation. All day long they play, in a world they make, without time or limitation. They call us to come back, to be children with them, still at play in a world we create.

www.dannyvaldes.com

Ordering Information:

Quantity sales. Special discounts are available on quantity purchases by corporations, associations, and others. For details, contact the publisher at the web address above.

Logo and brand design: Lisa Valdes

What if you could / Danny Valdes.
p. cm.

ISBN-13: 978-1-7331111-0-2

First Edition

PRINTED IN THE UNITED STATES OF AMERICA

What would this book be without the help and support of many, many people. These people are priceless. I knew nothing about publishing a book and I will admit, it was way harder than I thought. From the time commitment to the logistic of getting the thing edited, formatted and printed correctly, it was a massive undertaking.

Eternal gratitude to my dream girl who has been the bravest, most courageous woman of all time. She seems to be limitless in her patience and understanding of the wild places I ask her to venture. Every year I ask her to go on a new, high risk adventure. She sacrifices her womanly due of security and stability simply because she loves and trusts me. I haven't earned it, nor do I deserve it, but I have her support and that's really all I need.

To my 4 children who have worked harder than me on this project in that they have sacrificed time with their daddy, waiting patiently for his words, "The book is finished". You guys are my daily reminders of what love is and how I am supposed to walk in this world.

Besides my dream girl, I'm not going to name names because that would make the thickness of this book too large to get these killer shipping deals from USPS. To you very special people I extend my deepest gratitude. Without you, no one would understand a word I wrote, nor would it look good on a page. You are skilled in arts I am unfamiliar with, and that is what makes a product deliverable to real people. The concept that was in my heart is now shippable to the world and that is because of you.

Thank you.